Military Tech

MILITARY WEAPONS

JULIA GARSTECKI

BLACK RABBIT BOOKS

Bolt is published by Black Rabbit Books
P.O. Box 3263, Mankato, Minnesota, 56002.
www.blackrabbitbooks.com

Marysa Storm, editor; Michael Sellner, designer;
Omay Ayres, photo researcher

Library of Congress Cataloging-in-Publication Data
Names: Garstecki, Julia, author.
Title: Military weapons / by Julia Garstecki.
Description: Mankato, Minnesota : Black Rabbit Books, [2018] | Series: Bolt. Military tech | Includes bibliographical references and index. | Audience: Grades 4-6. | Audience: Ages 9-12.
Identifiers: LCCN 2016049973 (print) | LCCN 2016050336 (ebook) | ISBN 9781680721676 (library binding) | ISBN 9781680722314 (e-book)
Subjects: LCSH: Military weapons–Juvenile literature.
Classification: LCC UF500 .G37 2018 (print) | LCC UF500 (ebook) | DDC 623.4–dc23
LC record available at https://lccn.loc.gov/2016049973

Printed in the United States at CG Book Printers,
North Mankato, Minnesota, 56003. 3/17

Image Credits

Airforce.mil/photos: Staff Sgt. Lealan Buehrer, 12–13; Airforce.mil/photos / Wikimedia.org: Senior Master Sgt. John S. Chapman, 15 (top); Alamy: U.S. Navy, 16; Xinhua, 19; Army.mil/photos: Pfc. Gary Silverman, 1; Seth LaCount, 32; Spc. Patrick Kirby, 3; Timothy L. Hale, 4–5; Dreamstime: fmua, 11 (background); Getty Images: JACK GUEZ, 25 (missile being fired); MENAHEM KAHANA, 23; http://russiancouncil.ru/: Unknown, 20; https://www.defense.gov/Media/Photo-Gallery: U.S. Air Force, 14; https://www.dvidshub.net/image / Wikimedia.org: Abigail Waldrop, 24–25 (rocket and background), 29; http://www.peosoldier.army.mil/ Wikimedia.org: Nemo5576, 28; Navy.mil/photos, Alexander Tidd, 10–11; Navy.mil/photos / Wikimedia.org, John F. Williams, 26–27; Shutterstock: adamziaja.com, 9; Alexyz3d, 25 (explosion); Colin Hutchings, 11; CreativeHQ, 31; Przemek Tokar, Cover; Wikimedia.org, U.S. Army, 6; Wikimedia.org, U.S. Air Force, 15 (bottom); NatanFlayer, 22
Every effort has been made to contact copyright holders for material reproduced in this book. Any omissions will be rectified in subsequent printings if notice is given to the publisher.

CONTENTS

CHAPTER 1

Weapons in ACTION

A soldier aims her gun. Then she pulls the trigger. But nothing happens. The gun has taken over.

The gun has a built-in computer. The computer measures distance. It checks wind speed. When the gun knows it can hit the target, it fires.

Choosing the Right Weapons

Soldiers use many types of weapons. Some are used against enemies that are nearby. Others have a long **range**. Soldiers must be ready to use the right weapons for a job.

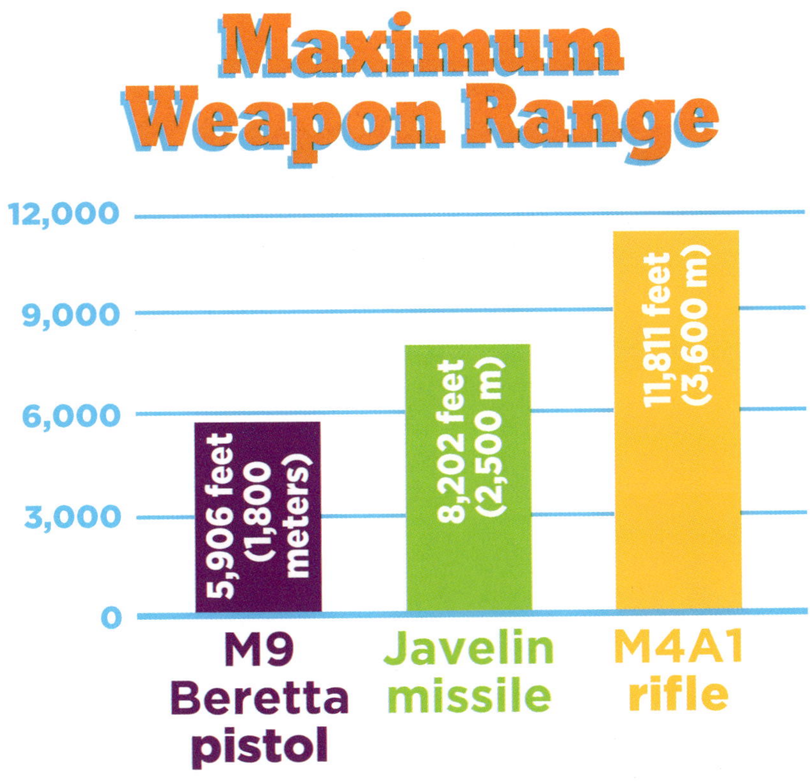

CHAPTER 2

WEAPONS
Carried by Soldiers

The M4A1 is a gun with many uses. Parts of the gun can change. It starts as a rifle. But it can turn into a **shotgun**. It can become a **grenade** launcher too. The M4A1 has a wide range. Targets can be nearby or far away.

U.S. Navy SEALs use the M4A1.

M4A1 By the Numbers

950
ROUNDS PER MINUTE

MAXIMUM RATE OF FIRE

14.5 INCHES
(37 CENTIMETERS)
barrel length

6.5
POUNDS
(3 KILOGRAMS)

WEIGHT OF M4A1

1,640 TO 11,811 FEET
(500 TO 3,600 M) RANGE

Hot or Cold

The M9 works when it's very hot or cold. It can fire at temperatures between -40 to 140 degrees Fahrenheit (-40 to 60 degrees Celsius).

Beretta M9

The M9 is a small pistol. It weighs around 2 pounds (1 kg). But it packs a punch. The gun fires bullets at around 1,200 feet (366 m) per second. It can take a beating too. The gun still fires after being buried in snow or sand. It can be dropped many times and still work too.

CHAPTER 3

Bombs and MISSILES

Sometimes armies need to attack large areas. That's when they use bombs.

Cluster bombs are containers full of little bombs. The little bombs are called bomblets.

Planes drop these bombs. As they fall, the containers open. The bomblets rain down on the ground below.

How Cluster Bombs Work

CLUSTER BOMB DROPS FROM PLANE

CONTAINER OPENS

BOMBLETS HIT GROUND

Cruise missiles fly near the ground. They are hard for radar to pick up. These missiles can be part of surprise attacks.

Cruise Missiles

Cruise missiles are guided bombs. Computers onboard tell them where to go. Systems scan land as missiles fly. They make sure missiles stay on track. Some missiles use cameras to make sure they hit their targets. Others use heat **sensors**.

Javelin Anti-Tank Missiles

Javelins are "fire and forget" missiles. They don't need any guiding. Before they're launched, the missiles lock onto their targets. Once fired, the weapons guide themselves. Soldiers just have to aim and fire.

Javelins are used against tanks and trucks. They can destroy small buildings too.

How Far ICBMs Can Go

R-36M (RUSSIA)

DF-5A (CHINA)

UGM-133 (UNITED STATES)

R-29RM (RUSSIA)

miles 0

Intercontinental Ballistic Missiles (ICBMs)

One type of missile beats the rest. It is the ICBM. These missiles are very powerful. They travel thousands of miles. Rocket engines power these long-range weapons.

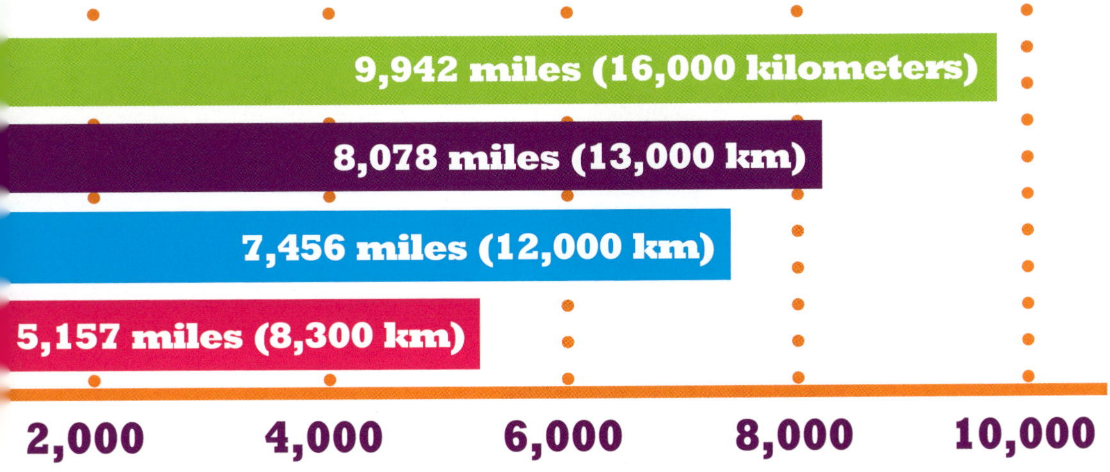

CHAPTER 4

Defense SYSTEMS

Many countries use **defense** systems to stay safe. These systems use radar to sense enemy rockets. The country then fires missiles. The missiles destroy enemy rockets.

THE IRON DOME DEFENSE SYSTEM

The Iron Dome defends the country of Israel.

MISSILE
GOES OFF NEAR
THE ROCKET
rocket
IS DESTROYED
missile
IS SHOT AT
THE ROCKET
STEP 3

CHAPTER 5

Weapons of the FUTURE

Militaries work to make their weapons better. They make new weapons too.

The U.S. military is working on laser weapons. Lasers are focused beams of light. They do damage by quickly heating targets. These weapons are quick and strong. Unlike missiles, they are quiet. In fact, lasers are silent. Lasers are cheaper than missiles too.

Faster and Stronger

As technology gets better, so do weapons. Weapons become faster. They become more powerful. Soldiers learn to use new weapons. They use them to protect their countries.

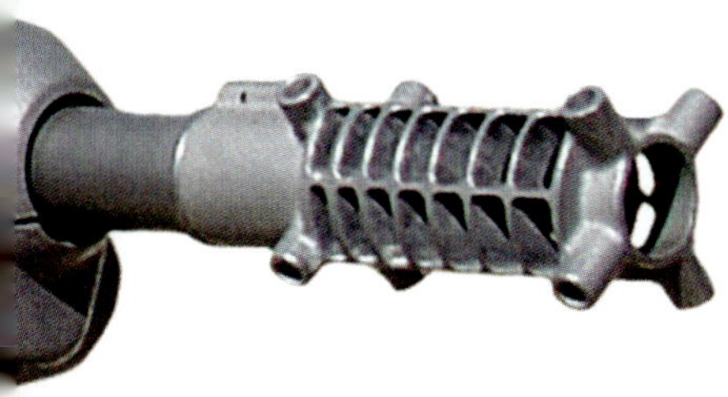

GLOSSARY

cluster (KLUHS-ter)—a group of things that are close together

cruise (KROOZ)—to move at a steady, easily controllable speed

defense (DEE-fens)—something that is used to protect someone or something from attack

grenade (greh-NAYD)—a small bomb

pistol (PIS-tl)—a small gun whose chamber is part of the barrel

radar (RAY-dar)—a device that sends out radio waves for finding the location and speed of a moving object

range (RAYNGE)—how far a weapon can go

rifle (RI-ful)—a shoulder weapon with grooves in the barrel

sensor (SEN-sor)—a device that detects heat, light, sound, motion, or other things

shotgun (SHAHT-gun)—a shoulder weapon with a smooth barrel used for firing at short ranges

LEARN MORE

BOOKS

Bow, James. *Lasers.* Cutting-Edge Technology. New York: Gareth Stevens Publishing, 2017.

Gagne, Tammy. *Incredible Military Weapons.* Ready for Military Action. Minneapolis: Core Library, an imprint of Abdo Publishing, 2015.

Nardo, Don. *In the Water: Torpedoes, Missiles, and Dive-Bombs.* The Military Experience. Greensboro, NC: Morgan Reynolds Pub., 2015.

WEBSITES

M4A1

navyseals.com/weapons-demo/m4a1/

M9

www.beretta.com/en-us/m9/

What Is a Laser?

spaceplace.nasa.gov/laser/en/

INDEX